TRUE TALES OF ENVIRONMENTAL MADNESS

TRUE TALES
OF
ENVIRONMENTAL
MADNESS

David Day & Tony Husband

PELHAM BOOKS

Stephen Greene Press

PELHAM BOOKS/Stephen Greene Press

Published by the Penguin Group
27 Wrights Lane, London W8 5TZ, England
Viking Penguin, a division of Penguin Books USA Inc
375 Hudson Street, New York, NY 10014, USA
The Stephen Greene Press Inc., 15 Muzzey Street, Lexington, Massachusetts 02173, USA
Penguin Books Australia Ltd, Ringwood, Victoria, Australia
Penguin Books Canada Ltd, 280-1 John Street, Markham, Ontario, Canada L3R 1B4
Penguin Books (NZ) Ltd, 182–190 Wairau Road, Auckland 10, New Zealand

Penguin Books Ltd, Registered Offices: Harmondsworth, Middlesex, England

First published 1990

Copyright © David Day and Tony Husband, 1990

Typeset in 11/13pt Century Old Style condensed by
Goodfellow & Egan Typesetting Ltd, Cambridge
Printed and bound by Richard Clay Ltd, Bungay, Suffolk.

A CIP catalogue record for this book is available from the British Library.

ISBN 0 7207 1974 7

CONTENTS

For the children: Stephen, Sean, Paul, Tarot, Charlotte, Edward, Gary, Elizabeth, Daniel.

ANIMAL ATTRACTION

Some may find it a peculiar way to make a living, but each day a research-worker straps a large black leather hat with a broad padded brim to his head and begins to do a little dance around the floor in a specially built loft. The dancer shakes, rocks and rolls his head until suddenly, a live peregrine falcon swoops down from its perch in the room and begins to make passionate love to the hat.

It's all in a day's work at the Cornell University captive falcon breeding programme. The reason for this bizarre activity is the near extinction of the peregrine falcon because of infertility caused by DDT poisoning. Cornell's plan was to find healthy birds and use artificial insemination techniques to increase their numbers. However, one of the main obstacles was a chronic shortage of sperm, which was notoriously difficult to coax out of the average male peregrine. It was found, however, that the mating process could be facilitated by human researchers simply duplicating the ritual courtship dance. With the advent of the mating hat specially equipped with a sperm reservoir, there was a hundred-fold increase in the acquisition of falcon sperm. The programme has been a resounding success, and a number of extinct regional populations have actually been restocked by these captive birds.

ARTICULATE APES

Between 1972 and 1982, Dr Penny Patterson taught a lowland gorilla, named Koko, a total of over 600 'words' in Ameslan (American Sign Language). Koko is certainly the most erudite ape the planet has yet seen. Koko's amazing vocabulary included many 'invented' words: 'finger-bracelet' for ring; 'bottle-match' for cigarette-lighter; 'nose-stink' for perfume; 'stuck-metal' for magnet. She also had creative curses; 'red-rotten-gorilla', 'red-rotten-mad', 'stupid-devil'. Like all 'talking' apes she also had a talent for scatological curses.

When Dr Patterson acquired a second gorilla called Michael, it was found the gorillas often carried on conversations quite independent of humans. Naturally enough this led to adolescent arguments. Koko rebuked the younger ape with: 'Michael dirty-toilet-devil'. Michael did not take this passively, he responded with the invective: 'Koko stink-bad, Squash-gorilla-lip.'

It also appeared that Michael had developed considerable skills as the class sneak. The laboratory cat's habits seemed of particular concern to Michael. When one or other of the researchers arrived in the morning, Michael couldn't wait to report: 'Cat cat chase eat bird . . .cat hit bad . . . cat bird frown hit-in mouth.' And some time later, almost like a little short story: 'Bird good cat chase eat red trouble cat eat bird.'

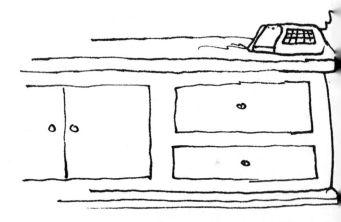

11

BAT BOMBS

In 1943, Dr Louis Feiser, a Harvard professor and the inventor of napalm, was instrumental in devising a new weapon for the US Army: the incendiary bat. To this end, thousands of bats were gathered from Carlsbad Caverns, New Mexico and Dr Feiser developed on incendiary device weighing about one ounce which could be surgically attached to the bat. The overall strategy was to airdrop tens of thousands of these live bat bombs over Japanese cities. The animals would fly into attics and belfreys and chew through the fuse-cord suturing. This would result in the napalm fire bombs igniting and burning down thousands of buildings in a single night. Development of the system, however, proved somewhat troublesome. There were numerous cases of premature cremation, one resulting in the burning down of a two million dollar US Army aircraft hangar. Still the researchers persisted and after more than two tumultuous years of development, the incendiary bat bomb was finally declared operational. However, by the time of its certification, the atom bomb was already on its way to Japan, and in the face of its massive destructive power, these miniature bombers proved to be redundant and unnecessary.

BAZOOKA DOGS

After horses, dogs are probably the most common auxiliary force attached to armies. In ancient and medieval times, some war hounds were even equipped with spiked collars and armour. In the First World War, dogs were primarily used as sentries, carriers of munitions, and tracking animals. The French had a particularly reliable network of dog messengers between front-line troops and officers – and consequently suffered more than five thousand casualties among its dog soldiers. (One of these well-trained trench dogs was rescued at the end of the war and taken back to America. He later emerged on the silver screen as the now-famous Rin-Tin-Tin.) The Russians came up with the most deadly use of the dog soldier. Using Pavlovian methods, they trained dogs loaded with high explosives to run under the belly of enemy tanks. The explosive pack on the dog's back had an extended antenna which, on striking the metal underside of the tank, triggered the detonator. The resulting explosion would destroy the tank; unfortunately it did not do the dog very much good either.

CACTUS VIGILANTE

In February of 1982, David M. Grundman, a 27-year-old Phoenix man, stood out in the Arizona desert in Manacopa County and fired repeated shotgun blasts into a giant saguaro cactus. (The large pitchfork-shaped saguaro cactus is Arizona's state plant and a protected endangered species. However, protection has proved almost impossible because of wide-spread destruction by collectors and vandals, and natural regeneration is slow.) The cactus Grundman fired on was 27-feet tall, only about half its maximum height. Standing a few feet away from the cactus, Grundman concentrated his fire about four feet up the base of the plant. When he let loose for a third time, the trunk suddenly gave way. To Grundman's surprise, the 23-foot upper section of the big cactus toppled directly on him. Grundman tried to step out of the way, but the cactus knocked the gunman to the ground with a vengeful force and perforated his body with thorns. Grundman arrived at the Phoenix Hospital looking like a human porcupine. He was pronounced dead-on-arrival.

COMPUTER CHIMP

Scientists of the Yerkes Regional Primate Research Center in Atlanta have developed a sturdy computer console which has been programmed with a computer language called Yerkish. In front of this computer panel, with its numerous keys in nine geometric shapes and seven colours, they placed a chimpanzee called Lana.

Lana proved an adept student. She soon learned sequential and grammatical structure on the console. A sentence would typically be typed into the computer: 'Please-machine-give-piece-of-banana,' or 'Please-Beverley-move-ball-into-room,' or 'Please-Tim-groom-Lana.' As the Yerkish inventors, Duane and Sue Rombough, noted: 'After a mere six months, Lana could complete correct sentence beginnings and cancel ungrammatical ones. Since then, Lana has demonstrated that she can do considerably more.'

Indeed she could – including basic mathematical calculations – but from the chimpanzee point of view (and even the human one), Yerkish is a sterile system of learning. Perhaps Lana herself has best demonstrated the limitations of mechanical teaching. When left alone in her room late one night, with only the computer for company, the lonely chimp plaintively typed in: 'Please-machine-tickle Lana.'

DESERT WAR

The war to stop the rapidly spreading desert regions of the world is being met head-on by some nations. Israel's systematic pushing back of the desert with elaborate irrigation schemes and tree-planting is well documented. Egypt and such places as Upper Volta are attempting to halt desert expansion by planting 'live fences': hedges of tough desert trees. Oil-rich Libya has come up with a bizarre scheme to stop expansion by paving the desert. Deep-rooted eucalyptus and acacia trees are planted on dunes. The dunes are then sprayed with a layer of asphalt in order to stop the desert sands from shifting and burying the new trees.

One of the grandest schemes is the current construction of a 'Great Green Wall of China': a wall of living trees planted roughly parallel to that greatest of the planet's man-made structures, the ancient stone Great Wall. The Green Wall is designed to protect the nation from the invasion of cold winds and sandstorms that blast out of Siberia and Mongolia which have helped to create vast tracts of desert. The Green Wall is part of a massive reforestation plan which will result in the planting of over a quarter-million square miles of trees by the year 2000.

DODO TREE

Dr Stanley Temple did not set out to become a green-thumbed saint; his real interest was in birds. However, something like the momentum of fate drew him to Mauritius. Here, Dr Temple became curious about the relationship between the extinct dodo bird and the tree Calvaria major which was endemic to Mauritius, but survived in only 13 living specimens. Once an extremely common native tree, its fruit was known to provide a major food source for the dodo and it consequently acquired the local name: dodo tree. But the relationship between the bird and the tree obviously went further, for not a single new sapling had grown since the dodo's extinction. All 13 remaining trees were in excess of 300 years old and nearing the end of their natural lifespan.

Determined to solve the riddle, Dr Temple played a hunch. He began by force-feeding a number of domestic turkeys with dodo tree fruit. He then dutifully gathered up the droppings, sorted out the fruit seeds (which he noted had been deeply scoured by their passage through the turkeys' gizzards) then planted them. The result was the germination of three seeds, and the sprouting of the first dodo tree saplings in three centuries. It is now believed that an artificial means of abrasion can be used to scour the thick seed-casing to prepare it for planting, and by this means the species will be saved from extinction.

ELEPHANT PARATROOPERS

During the Vietnam War, American strategists found that elephants were the only means the South Vietnamese and Hill Tribe allies had of carrying heavy equipment and supplies through certain jungle and swamp regions. Undeterred by a shortage of elephants in the war zones, the US military soon put together an elephant paratrooper division. Soon, tranquillised elephants were dropped by parachute from huge transport planes into combat zones.

In 1968, when this updated version of Hannibal's March was discovered by a few members of the press, an animal cruelty charge was levelled at the American army over the issue. A military attaché firmly and categorically denied the charge. The animals were, after all, tranquillised, and sending them by air was in fact a great kindness. It spared them 'a long walk through the jungle'.

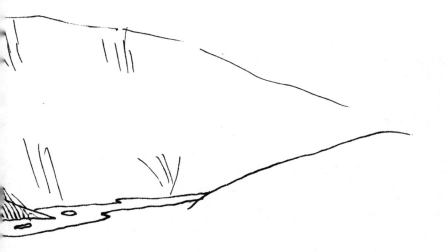

EXECUTIONER CROCODILES

Few people would categorize Idi Amin as a conservationist. However, it is impossible to deny the fact that during Idi Amin's dictatorship, Uganda was the only region in the world where the crocodile population did not decline. True, Amin slaughtered virtually every other species under his stewardship: he was especially notable for his destruction of elephants, which he virtually exterminated in Uganda by sending military helicopter gunships into national parks to slaughter for their ivory. Nevertheless, Amin did have a soft spot for crocodiles. As he himself pointed out, he was the saviour of the African crocodile and Uganda has become 'the crocodile capital of the world' under his guiding hand. During his time at the helm of government, the crocodiles of Uganda experienced a population explosion. Curiously enough, the rise in the Ugandan crocodile population was proportionately equal to the decline in the numbers of Amin's human subjects and political enemies.

FASHION VICTIMS

The 'wild' fur trade – much of it illegal – has critically endangered all species of striped and spotted cats. This billion-dollar fashion-fur industry has been responsible for the decimation of nearly every fur-bearing species it has chosen to exploit. Import controls are something of a joke: in one typical year official world export figures for wild cat skins was 60,000, and yet customs records for West Germany alone showed that over 300,000 wild cat skins were imported that same year. The wild fur and skin market has been responsible for the extinction of three races of tigers, three races of bears, a dozen or more races of wolves, the Caribbean Monk Seal and the giant Sea Mink, among others. The only native mammal on the Falkland Islands was also a fashion victim in the late nineteenth century. This was a strange animal called the 'Antarctic Wolf-Fox' or Falkland Island 'Aquara Dog'. The Astor family furriers of New York became interested in this large wolf-fox with a luxurious coat. Soon, the Astor furriers were proudly advertising a 'last opportunity clearance sale' of wolf-fox furs. This was quite literally true; they had made a total clearance of the species. The last animal was shot and skinned in Shallow Bay in Hill Cove Canyon in 1876 – the last casualty in the short-lived Falklands Fur Wars.

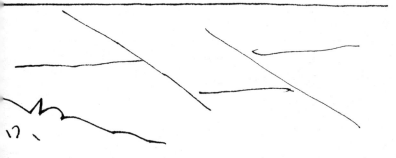

FLIM FLAM ANIMALS

Exotic animal traders are notorious for ingenious frauds which exploit gullible, uninformed buyers. Even when they trade with supposedly well-informed animal handlers and zoos, they manage to pull off an astounding range of fraudulent techniques. Dealers commonly sell large numbers of highly-priced baby leopards which never seem to grow. In fact, the animals are bengal cats: small, inexpensive felines that never weigh more than 4 kilos. Many kinds of reasonably common birds and animals are used as substitutes for related, but more expensive, species. One dealer went so far as to invent a species called the 'Golden Panther', which was actually the fairly common Temminck's cat, but because of its unique status he increased its price tenfold.

Some dealers have a capacity for audacity that puts the salesman in the *Monty Python* 'Dead Parrot' sketch to shame. Petshop owners who are conned into pre-paying for merchandise often find they have entire shipments made up of such exotics as: limbless alligators, three-legged cats, paraplegic aardvarks, furless otters, and featherless birds. Sometimes the dealers are slightly more subtle in defrauding their customers. In the cases of some of the larger mammals which are expensive to purchase, but breed easily in captivity, traders often manage to double or triple their profits by making the animals sterile. In the case of large ungulates, like the wild camels, the method used is crushing the testicles with clapboards, a mutilation almost impossible to detect. When a buyer eventually finds his animals are sterile, suspecting nothing, he simply reorders from the same trader in the hope of getting a fertile group.

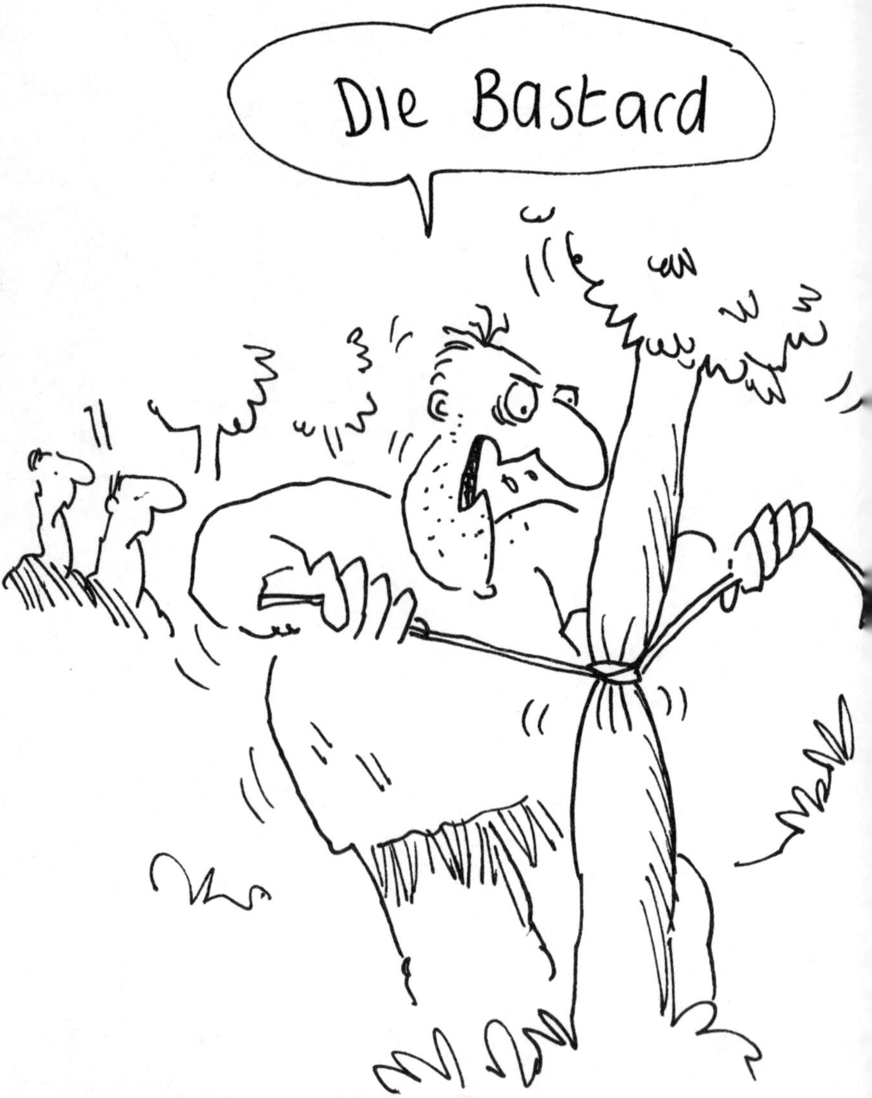
Die Bastard

GARROTTING THE WINE PALM

In the past two centuries an estimated ten thousand vascular plant species have become extinct due to man's depredations. Among them have been considerable numbers of decorative plants; victims of cactus rustlers, orchid smugglers and other breeds of black market plant merchants. Most species, however, have been eliminated by over-exploitation or habitat destruction. The Hawaiian islands, for instance, are known to have lost at least 300 unique species, and another 800 are endangered.

Many of extinct species were extremely valuable. The beautiful Mauritian ebony and the fragrant Juan Fenandez sandalwood are two valuable trees which were needlessly extinguished by timber merchants. Another was the beautiful wine palm of Dominica. This was so named because of the fine clear wine that could be made from its pleasant juicy sap. The tree also produced a cherry-like fruit. Unfortunately, instead of tapping the tree for its sap as is done with the sugar maple tree, or the rubber tree, the preferred method of extraction was a kind of garrotting process. This, however entirely cut off the flow of life-giving sap and invariably killed the tree. Through ludicrous over-exploitation, the last Dominican wine palm was garrotted in 1926, and the species became extinct.

GREAT EGG ROBBERY

The British Natural History Museum's ornithological division at Tring has the finest and largest collection of rare bird specimens in the world. It also boasts a collection of over a million eggs from rare and exotic species. In 1978, one regular amateur researcher was taken to one side by security guards at the exit door of the museum. A search of the suspect soon revealed that beneath his loose-fitting trousers he wore a woman's pantihose stuffed with a large number of rare eggs. Subsequent investigators discovered that this man – over a period of two years – had engineered the greatest robbery of rare eggs in the annals of oviparous crime. When an audit was made, it was discovered that the man had stolen no less than 30,000 eggs! The thief was a full-time professional egg bandit who was a major trader in an illegal egg-collectors' black market. He was eventually sentenced to nearly two years in prison, but the museum staff were sentenced to decades of frustration as they attempted to restore the collection to some semblance of order. Not only did the thief steal irreplaceable eggs, but he 'contaminated' every section entered by changing markings and switching labels. Unfortunately, the museum's desire to minimise embarrassment over this disaster seems greater than its desire to expose those who remain major players in this egg smugglers' black market network.

IN MEMORY OF
SUPER
HAMSTER
THE
FATHER
OF A
NATION

HECTIC HAMSTER HISTORY

Once a species becomes critically endangered, bringing it back from near extinction to a healthy and viable state is nearly always a long and slow struggle against formidable odds. But, there have been a few quite spectacular rebounds from the edge of oblivion. Perhaps the greatest zoological comeback of all time occurred in 1930, when a Palestinian scholar named Professor Aharoni embarked on a personal quest to the ruined ancient Hittite city of Chaleb (now called Aleppo) to look for signs of 'a special kind of Syrian mouse' which he had read about in ancient Aramaic texts. It had been a domestic pet in antiquity, but it was obviously a creature that was, as yet, unknown to modern science.

However, soon after arriving at the site of the ancient city, instead of merely finding skeletons of the creatures, the professor actually stumbled across a burrow alive with 13 of these unique red-gold rodents. Professor Aharoni had discovered the world's only surviving population of what is now the common household pet called the golden hamster. No one has ever recorded sighting these animals in the wild before, or since. Extraordinary as it may seem, the world's entire population of perhaps 50 million golden hamsters are all descended from those original 13 industrious little beasts unearthed by the curious scholar in ancient Chaleb.

HUMANE HUNTING

American television's 'NBC Today Show' received more abusive letters and phone calls than at any time in its history after the guest appearance of Cleveland Amory, the flamboyant president of the 'Fund For Animals'. Amory, a self-confessed 'humaniac' and an outspoken advocate of 'the right to arm bears', announced that he was forming a new club called: 'The Hunt the Hunters Hunt Club'. It boasted the motto: 'If you can't play a sport, shoot one.' It was not, he pointed out, an attempt to exterminate hunters, but simply a culling to 'trim the herd'.

The club would demand strict enforcement of rules: bow hunters to be shot with arrows, fox hunters to be ridden down on horseback with only pure-bred dogs, trappers to be trapped – humanely, of course. Naturally there would be sportsmanlike controls. 'Please do not, for instance, simply go out and take pot shots at hunters – within city limits, say, or in parked cars, or in their dating season.'

One must also be tactful. After bagging a hunter, for example, the club advises against draping the corpse over the automobile in an ostentatious fashion – particularly in an area where relatives of the bagged hunter are likely to be found. Members were also advised that 'mounting heads is considered by the club to be in very bad taste.'

Finally, Amory mentioned the concern expressed by some members about the reputed toughness of many hunters. This was patently untrue. 'Properly prepared and seasoned', Amory assured his viewers, 'they can be quite tasty.'

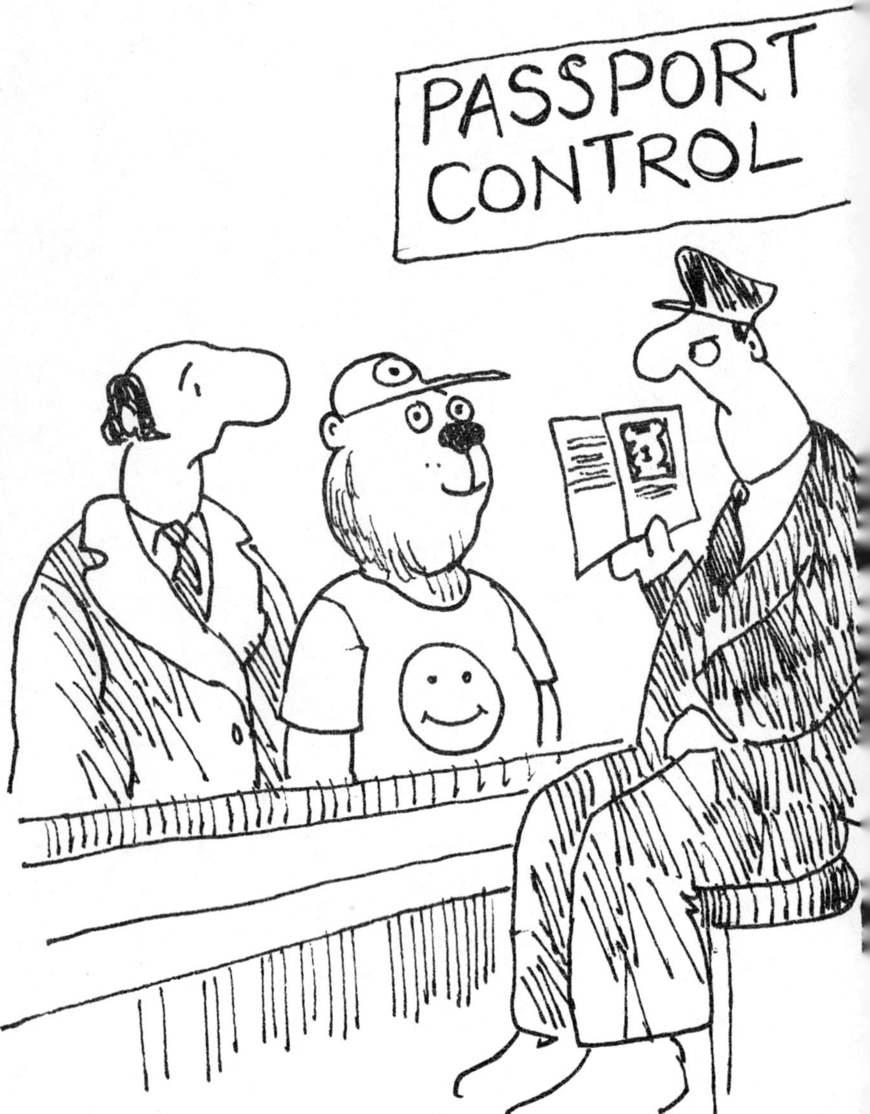
PASSPORT
CONTROL

ILLEGAL IMMIGRANTS

High market prices for rare and exotic live animals for zoos, circuses and the pet trade has made animal smuggling a highly profitable occupation. The reformed South-east Asian animal smuggler Jean-Yves Domalain confessed he had smuggled: gibbons, clouded leopards, black leopards, douc monkeys, and many species of birds. All of the thousands of animals he handled were illegal. It was Domalain's belief and experience that the 'legal' wild-captured animal is almost non-existent. In excess of 90 per cent of all wild-captured animals are illegal.

Hunters virtually never have permits, middlemen virtually never have legitimate papers, either for import or customs. Most live animals are smuggled through official channels by a combination of outright bribery and forged documents. At Bangkok, Bogota and Nairobi airports the going rate is between twenty and a hundred dollars a crate.

On the import side – in Europe and America – where bribery of officials is less common, forged or stolen documents with official stamps and signatures are often used. Also, as few customs inspectors can tell one exotic cat, monkey or bird species from another, illegal species are mixed up with legal ones. In more obvious cases, cages with dual compartments are used, with the illegal species hidden beneath. Particularly unpopular creatures like scorpions or poisonous snakes are the only visible species, so detailed inspection seldom goes beyond a quick visual search.

INVADER CATFISH

Over the past four centuries, Europeans have introduced scores of species into the newly 'discovered' world with devastating effect. Rats, cats and dogs have decimated or – in over a hundred cases – entirely exterminated New World birds and mammals. Horses, cattle and sheep have driven out other grazing beasts. Pigs, goats and rabbits have converted lush tropic islands into deserts. The Hawaiian islands, in common with many tropic islands, have lost two-thirds of their birds through the introduction of aggressive European species contaminated with fatal diseases like avian malaria.

Some introduced species have been very strange indeed. In Florida, in the mid-1960s, the 'Walking Catfish' from south-east Asia was imported to fish farms as a novelty. This large, bizarre and very tough fish is capable of climbing out of its pond and moving overland to other pools or streams. It is a tenacious and aggressive fish, and there are many accounts of family dogs being badly bitten while investigating the curious spectacle of a 'walking' fish. By 1970, it had managed to infiltrate almost every pond and waterway in Florida, and push out all competitors. When last seen, the 'Walking Catfish' was relentlessly marching north and west in its finny conquest of America.

BEWARE
OF THE
FISH

GPO

JUNGLE GRAFFITI

Strangely enough, besides the notably high percentage of criminals and swindlers to be found in the ranks of the exotic animal trafficking fraternity, there appears to be a more sensitive, artistic element. These are the professional 'wildlife painters' of this shady business. In their way, they might argue that they are real artists of considerable experience, for they don't bother with the interim medium of canvas when they paint an animal: they actually paint the live animal itself. Considerable numbers of tropical birds, for instance, are painted or colour dyed to improve the brightness of their feathers. Often, in fact, they transform the birds into a related – but far more expensive – species. Otters and other fairly common animals often have their fur bleached with peroxide. These are labelled 'albinos' and are sold for 20 or 30 times their ordinary value.

The aerosol spray paint can is also in wide use among this same breed of jungle artist who commonly attempts to improve on nature by spray painting an astonishing array of exotic plant and animal species to increase their trade value. One trader simply used aerosol spray paint to convert his common leopards into rarer – and much more expensive – black leopards. Unfortunately, besides being ozone-unfriendly, this use of aerosols often proves deadly. Most of these CFC addicts don't bother to check out the kind of paint they are using. Often, the paint proves to be toxic and when the animal attempts to lick or preen the paint off, it is fatally poisoned.

Sorry pal but when you asked if I could re-spray a jaguar
BERTS RESPRAYS

JUNGLE WARFARE

Jungle warfare took on a new meaning during the Vietnam conflict when the Americans decided to wage war on the jungle itself. A division of 'Anti-Forest Rangers' were established to eliminate vast tracts of forest land used by Viet Cong troops with a lethal combination of napalm and a chemical defoliant called Agent Orange. These Anti-Forest Rangers used a parody of Smokey the Bear's fire prevention message as their corps motto: 'Only WE can prevent forests.'

However, the 'scorched earth' tactics of jungle warfare continue today in only a slightly less flamboyant manner than during the Vietnam War years. At a rate of an area equal to one Cuba a year, the rainforests are coming down, and the world's 200 million tribal peoples are being displaced. This is as true in the Amazon, as it is in the Phillipines, Borneo and the Solomon Islands. In each place, it is a battlefield typically seen as a 'blowpipes against bulldozers' conflict.

Everywhere it is clear that the chainsaw massacre of the rainforests is out of control. In Thailand, pirate logging companies actually highjack trains to haul their illegal timber to market. They command private armies and are openly at war with the government. In one year over a thousand Thais died and tens of thousands were left homeless when illegally logged-off mountains turned to seas of mud and slid down and buried schools, hospitals, roads and villages.

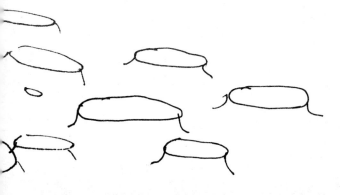

KAMIKAZE CATS

The Kamikaze Cat Squadrons were the brainchild of the wartime OSS (Office of Strategic Services), the forerunner of the CIA, under the guidance of British Intelligence. The idea was to seek ways of improving the accuracy of American bombs being dropped on Japanese ships. The Japanese Kamikazes had proved how dangerous a dedicated pilot could be. However, human rights being what they were in America, the US military grudgingly concluded it would need substitutes for human pilots in their own flying bombs. Operating on the principle: 'Why think when you can experiment?', one series of experiments developed a guided bomb system involving cats. The basic idea was to strap cats into explosive backpack devices and drop them from high altitude bombers. The logic behind this experiment was that a cat's natural hatred of water would result in it doing anything it possibly could to land on the (dry) deck of the enemy ship rather than land in the (very wet) sea. It soon became fairly obvious to most observers of this experiment that fear of wet paws was not uppermost in the minds of the terrified cats as they plunged several thousand feet down towards the earth with bombs strapped to their backs. Not surprisingly, The Kamikaze Cat Squadron did not prove to be a major triumph for the strategic genius who dreamt it up.

KILLER CHEMICALS

In the American Pacific Northwest, chemical spraying over vast forest regions has caused major protest programmes and acts of ecotage after evidence of genetic damage to unborn children was demonstrated. Expressing the sentiment of many about spraying over-populated areas, Friends of the Earth wrote a letter to federal authorities; 'I would like to suggest', the letter read, 'that if it is legal to spray people with poison from aircraft and ground rigs without their permission, it should also be quite legal for anyone, including spray victims, to walk into your offices with pesticide cans and spray you with poisons.'

In many Third World nations the issue was extremely volatile. One might use Guatemala's one million cotton plantation farm workers as an example. With no safety measures whatever, they suffer incidental pesticide spraying approximately 50 times a season as they work in the fields. This results in thousands of workers suffering from vomiting, dizziness and delirium. Many become so severely ill, they die. Worldwide, a million people a year are seriously poisoned by pesticides, and at least 5,000 of these actually die.

It is not surprising that vigilante actions are increasing. Provoked beyond endurance, a group called the 'Guatemalan Army of the Poor' went on the rampage. In a single night, they burned and destroyed no fewer than 22 crop-dusting planes.

So let's see if I've got this right. She can be any age between 5 and 250. Non-smoker, likes swimming, slow walks and must have a full bodied shell...ok?

COMPUTA-DATE AGENCY

LONESOME TURTLES

The Charles Darwin Research Station on the Galapagos Islands is the home of the last living specimen of the Abingdon Island Giant Tortoise. Since 1957, this solitary male has been the last tortoise of his species. For over thirty years, 'Lonesome George' – as he is generally known – has wandered dolefully around the research station while the resident scientists have been running 'lonely heart' column ads in zoological magazines with the hope that some animal collector somewhere in the world still has a surviving female Abingdon Giant Tortoise.

The future doesn't look all that good for Lonesome George, although the station probably does have another hundred years to resolve the problem. Nobody really knows how long Giant Tortoises live, but there is a living Giant Tortoise on Tonga which local people claim was presented to the King of Tonga in 1774 by Captain James Cook! Although it is not possible to confirm this animal's age, there is the authenticated case of Marion's Giant Tortoise. This animal was taken as a fully grown adult from the Seychelles to the French garrison on Mauritius by the Chevalier Marion de France in the year 1776. Sadly, like Lonesome George, Marion's Tortoise was the last lonely animal of its species. He remained Port Louis' garrison mascot until 1918, when he died of unnatural causes.

After 152 years of mateless captivity, who could blame him for being frustrated and a little depressed. It seems that inexplicably one morning he woke earlier than usual and decided to climb the garrison battlements. Once up on them, he seems to have deliberately walked off one of the parapets and toppled to his death.

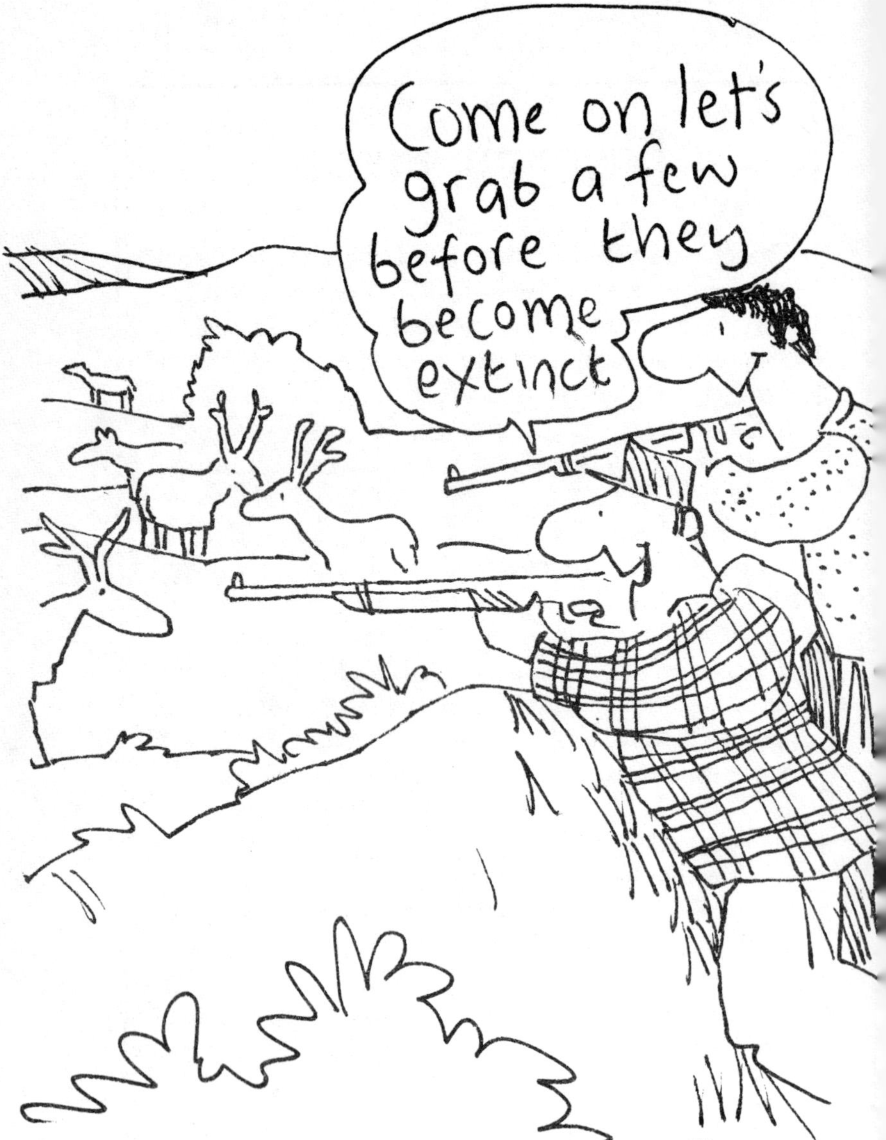
Come on let's grab a few before they become extinct

MIDGET REINDEER

There has been a considerable number of very peculiar extinctions on this planet during the last two centuries. The Huia bird of New Zealand, for instance, became extinct because George V stuck a couple of its feathers in his hatband and established a fashion craze that wiped them out. The last Eastern American Elk were obliterated because the masonic brotherhood of the Fraternal Order of the Elks used its canine teeth as a watch-chain insignia. The Shamanu or Japanese Miniature Wolf was extinguished because of a superstition that it had the supernatural powers of a vampire or werewolf. Shomburgk's Siamese Deer was finished off by hunters who believed its antlers had aphrodesiac qualities. And New Zealand's tiny, flightless bird called the Stephen Island Wren was entirely wiped out by a single lighthouse-keeper's cat.

The Dwarf Caribou of British Columbia, however, is the only species to have been the victim of an academic debate. For a number of years, there were conflicting stories about the animal on B.C.'s Queen Charlotte Islands. Some scientists supported this theory with a few antlers reputedly brought from the islands, while others claimed these originated elsewhere and argued that no caribou could survive in this island habitat. Finally, the debate escalated to such an extent that the academics offered a large bounty for physical evidence. An expedition was launched and culminated when the bounty hunters stumbled onto what proved to be the last surviving herd. Of course, they shot the entire herd. The Dwarf Caribou has the dubious distinction of being simultaneously discovered and extinguished in the same cataclysmic moment.

MINESWEEPER PIGS

Since World War I, dogs have been trained to sniff out mines and other buried explosives. However, U.S. Army experiments have found that a number of other animals have superior sniffing power; racoons, cats, ferrets and skunks. However, the absolute champion is the domestic red duroc pig. It is capable of smelling out explosives at four times the depth that a dog can detect them. However, the Army has had great difficulty recruiting potential trainers. Some soldiers, it seems, feel it is rather undignified to become known as a pig-trainer. Similarly, in civil situations, police bomb squads find it almost impossible to find an officer willing to walk around with a pig on a lead.

Nuclear whales

The US Navy has trained white beluga whales, pilot whales and killer whales to perform numerous underwater errands for its operations. One of these is the retrieval of test-fired nuclear torpedoes and other lost equipment. For shallow waters, beluga white whales were found effective; for depths to 850 ft killer whales were employed; and for depths down to 1650 ft, pilot whales were employed. Although these trained whales are considered extremely reliable retrievers, one killer whale is known to have deserted in an open water exercise with about a half-a-million dollars' worth of military technology strapped to him. He was never seen again. 'Was he working for the Russians all along?' asked one trouble-making journalist trying to stir up military paranoia. There is little doubt that whales are also being developed for more aggressive purposes and have been trained to carry explosives. One scientist working for the military claims research is being conducted to use whales to track Russian Nuclear Submarines.

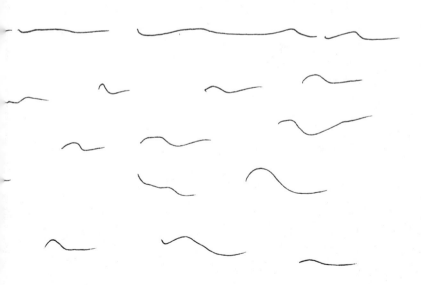

ONASSIS BARSTOOLS

Even by the cut-throat standards of international whaling of the 1950's, Aristotle Onassis was in a class of his own. Onassis's outlaw fleet particularly irritated the Norwegians, the great whalers of the day. The manager of the Onassis fleet was a disgraced member of the Norwegian Nazi Party; the company agent was the administrator of Norway's whaling ships for Nazi Germany; the overall commander of all eighteen ships was Captain Wilhelm Reichert, formerly of the Third Reich's navy, and most of the crew were German ex-military or Norwegian turncoats. It turned out to be an ideal combination, of course. It was the world's largest pirate whaling company and – by ignoring quotas and closed seasons, by hunting in restricted waters, and slaughtering protected species, nursing mothers and suckling young – it trounced all its competitors.

Flamboyant in the extreme, Onassis took many famous guests on board his ships and invited them (in dinner jacket or evening dress) to fire harpoons into dying whales. On his yacht 'Christina', the bar was fitted with whale ivory and sported bar stools made from the penises of sperm whales. The point of this exercise in taxidermy was made evident on one famous occasion when the great Greta Garbo slid up to the bar. Invited to take a seat, she was graciously informed: 'Miss Garbo, you are now sitting on the world's largest penis.'

Orchid smugglers

It appears that almost anything rare and exotic has a price on its head. This is as true in the plant kingdom as it is in the animal world. There is a large and flourishing illegal trade in endangered plants, just as there is in endangered animals.

High on the list of commercially exploitable plants are orchids. Thanks to worldwide air transport, extremely rare orchids can be taken from the jungle and flown to markets around the world in a couple of days. As a result, thousands of rare orchid species are rapidly achieving endangered status in their jungle habitats of India, Latin America, South-East Asia and the South Pacific. In India, at least ten species are known to have become extinct in recent years through this trade, and a score or more are certain to disappear in the next few years.

Many other ornamental plants have also been seriously threatened. Besides the orchids, the next most seriously threatened group is the cactus family. In America 'cactus-rustling', as it is known, has become a multi-million dollar black-market industry. The desert environment has been so severely looted that in 1980, Arizona appointed a seven-man force of 'cactus cops'. However, with prices ranging anywhere from $25 to $1000 a cactus, profits are considerable for some rustlers and interference by the cactus cops has resulted in a number of gunfights.

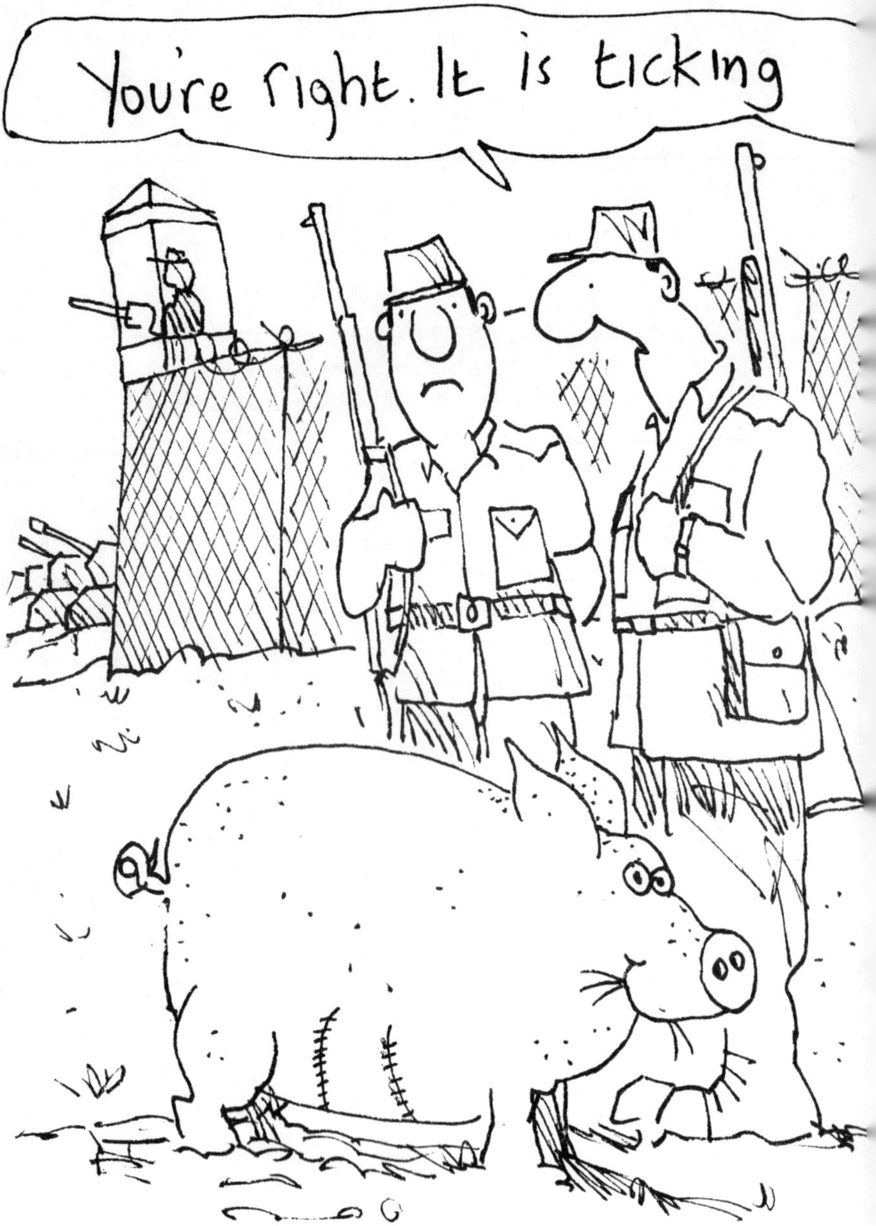
You're right. It is ticking

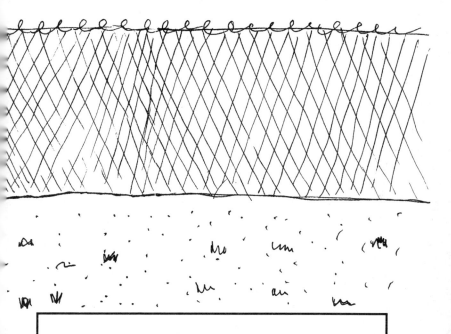

PIG BOMBS

A number of experiments for the U.S. armed forces during the past few decades have resulted in recruitment of the pig in a more aggressive military role: that of a walking bomb. Under defence contracts, the Animal Behavior Enterprises Laboratories have conducted implant operations on large pigs. The experiments demonstrate that pigs can be implanted with up to 23 lbs of explosives. The pig can then be trained to infiltrate enemy barracks or camps, and exploded by remote control devices.

PIGEON-GUIDED MISSILES

Possibly the most bizarre use of pigeons in warfare was the one devised by the father of behaviourist psychology, B.F. Skinner during WW II. Skinner had been contracted to develop a guidance system for the problematic US Navy 'Pelican' missiles. The 'Pelican' seemed to have no gyroscopic balance and very little sense of direction either: two considerable drawbacks for a supposedly 'guided' missile.

Skinner's solution to the clumsy Pelican was simplicity itself: put a homing pigeon in the nose cone. Balance problems would be resolved by the fact that a pigeon's inner ear mechanism works like a gyroscope and the bird always balances itself and remains upright. Meanwhile, the direction of the missile could be corrected by continuous pecking by the bird at a target image projected through a lens system. Experiments simulating the 660 mph missile dive on a target ship demonstrated fairly conclusively that the pigeons could act with absolute accuracy as a guidance system.

However, although Project Orcon ('Organic Control') was declared operational, the system was not put to practical use against the Japanese navy. This, Skinner sadly concluded, was because of the military officers' prejudices and anticipated ridicule about the Navy being controlled by 'bird brains'. Somehow, the whole idea was seen as being rather too low-tech and un-American.

Quarrels in the Quagmire

On 27 March 1983, three investigators for the Environmental Investigation Agency in Atlanta, acting on a tip about an illegal toxic waste dump site, were searching the Alabama woodlands. They soon discovered the dump site: huge stacks of rusting and leaking fifty-five gallon drums of chemical waste. As they began to investigate the degree of contamination on the site, gunfire suddenly erupted around them and they found themselves huddling behind the chemical drums for shelter. When the gunshots subsided, the unarmed agents fled the scene.

That same year, there were numerous violent incidents in New York, Philadelphia and Houston which resulted in federal agents being badly beaten, attacked by dogs, and shot at. In Seattle there were fire bombings and in Chicago death threats silenced informers and trial witnesses in toxic dumping cases.

As the EPA itself points out, since 90 per cent of all toxic waste is dumped illegally or unsafely, chemical garbage has become big business in the world of organized crime. Large criminal organizations are deeply involved in garbage and toxic waste, and 1983 marked the beginning of a new violent era when these organizations have made efforts to protect their interests. Violent confrontations have increased and evidence of their poison hand is everywhere. In 1989, for instance, it was discovered that for nearly a decade American organized crime has been disposing of a number of dangerous toxic chemicals by simply mixing them into legally sold fuel oil which is then sold for domestic and industrial use. Thus private homes, hospitals, schools, factories, even large cargo and passenger ships are unknowingly responsible for the spread of airborne toxic wastes over their communities.

Yer gonna get wasted pal... get it waste... toxic... Ha Ha funny eh?
POP
POP

RUSSIAN SPORTSMEN

In March 1982, a forest ranger named Valery Rinchinov was shot dead by illegal night hunters on a nature preserve near Lake Baikal, Siberia. It was a major embarrassment when the killers were found to be communist party officials. However, it was not an unusual scenario. Soviet preserves are commonly (and illegally) used by the military and communist party-members for 'sport' hunting and as a source of black-market meat and furs. The Soviet magazine 'Literaturnaya Gazeta' has reported scores of deaths in pitched battles between game wardens and Soviet soldiers who use helicopters, automatic weapons and hand grenades to poach deer, boar, tiger, bear and wild sheep. One military commander, Marshall Batitskii, was noted for his weekend hobby of machine-gunning 'protected' polar bears from helicopter gunships.

One particularly audacious illegal party hunt was led by Marshall Chuikov into the Kyzl-Agach preserve in a column of military all-terrain vehicles, communication cars and field kitchens. At dawn the vehicles were tearing across the banks and shallows, blasting away at ducks, geese and teal. After a break for lunch, Chuikov and his comrades transferred to helicopters and swooped down on herds of deer and wild boar as the 'sportsmen' shot to their hearts' content with heavy-gauge automatic rifles. In the end, tanks were brought into the preserve in order to drag the other vehicles and their booty out of the 'protected' swamp lands of the preserve.

SAGEBRUSH TERRORISTS

The Wild West tradition in the Western U.S. has given birth during the last decade to a radical organization of self-confessed 'sagebrush terrorists'. The organization is called 'Earth First!' and its symbol is a clenched green fist. Earth First! is modelled on the activist philosophy of a fictional group called 'The Monkey Wrench Gang' from a novel of that title by Edward Abbey.

The group issues its own newspaper and a number of DIY booklets on ecotage. One is titled 'Ecodefence: A Field Guide to Monkey Wrenching', and is an instruction manual on how to dismantle billboards, spike trees, sabotage roads, destroy bridges, disable helicopters, burn bulldozers – and make a clean get-away.

Drawing widespread support from rural working-class westerners, Earth-Firsters often proudly call themselves 'Rednecks For Wilderness'. They argue you don't need a doctorate to understand the wilderness is being raped.

Although most ecology groups condemn Earth-Firster tactics, they are not without supporters. The legendary founder of Friends of the Earth, David Brower, has often spoken in their defence. 'These people are not the terrorists,' says Brower. 'The real terrorists are the polluters and despoilers of nature.' Brower seems in agreement with the veteran Earth-Firster, Dave Foreman, on ecotage: 'It's one tool. Sometimes you lobby; sometimes you write letters; sometimes you file lawsuits. And sometimes you monkey wrench.'

Well bring it here Thompson. There's a message tied to it
VERY BIG INDUSTRIES LTD
CHAIRM

SINGING WHALES

In 1970, the largest single pressing of any phonographic record in history was made. Capitol Records, in co-operation with *National Geographic*, produced ten million copies. Remarkably the recording artists who merited this mass publication were totally unknown to the public. Even more remarkably, the singers were not even human.

The record was a smash hit. The humpback whale overnight became the world's greatest recording artist. The 'Songs of the Humpback Whale' were collected by Dr Roger Payne, who described the humpback as the greatest 'singer' among the whales. Why humpback whales should sing is not really known, but it is obviously a form of communication. Whales sing songs solo, in duets, in trios, in quartets and in entire school choruses.

Whale songs are like human dialects. All whales in one place will sing one dialect, while their cousins in another breeding ground will sing a completely different arrangement. Songs change and evolve very gradually over weeks and months, in length and timing. Dr Payne equates these changes with musical 'themes' in symphonies, to use a simpler analogy, with songs that have 'musical rounds' which are dropped out, split apart and rearranged. After a time all phrasing is gradually replaced and a completely new song emerges. As Dr Payne stated: 'The whales use a technique very much like a good composer uses to create beautiful and interesting music'.

TREE HUGGERS

In 1733, a young peasant girl in the mountainous north of India embraced a tree in an attempt to block the maharajah's axemen who were to cut down the forest near her village. Unfortunately, this action did not stop the axemen. The young martyr was killed along with 363 other village-tree-huggers before the maharajah relented and granted the villagers the right to maintain their own forest resources. This is the historical precedent for a grass-roots peasant protest movement which was formed in Uttar Pradesh in 1973. It is called 'Chipko Andolan' or the 'Hugging Movement' – 'chipko' meaning 'embrace'. The Chipko people know that their subsistence economy depends on the survival of the forests. Consequently, when timber companies attempt to open a new area to logging, the Chipko demonstrators – the majority of whom are women – literally throw themselves in front of the chainsaws and hug the trees. In many instances the tree huggers' tactics have paid off. A meeting between Chipko leader Sunderlal Bhaunguna and Indira Ghandhi resulted in the 1981 government ban in cutting trees above the 3,300 foot level in the Himalayas. Furthermore the movement is spreading. Wherever the Chipko organizers go they spread their message of forest ecology: 'What do the forests bear? Soil, water and pure air.'

Don't worry Margaret. If it can work in Uttar Pradesh, it can damn well work in Chipping-cum-Sodbury
CHANNEL TUNNEL LINK ROAD

Trojan toucans

Wildlife traffickers in South America and Asia have formed alliances with drug traffickers to their mutual benefit. The operations manifest themselves in many bizarre variations. Typical of these is the 'trojan toucan': a shipment of several hundred live toucans or parrots are shipped out of Colombia into the U.S. through the usual channels. However, a dozen have been killed and stuffed with cocaine. Since it is not uncommon for as many as half of the birds to die in transit, customs officers see nothing unusual. Upon arrival, the smugglers simply slit open the birds and remove the drugs. In South-East Asia, the cages and boxes made to ship some of the fiercer carnivores and jungle cats were often made of laminated wood filled with heroin. This proved a reliable system; not many customs inspectors are particularly keen to check the floorboards of a tiger's shipping crate. Probably the all-time best drug smugglers are the pythons. It is relatively easy to persuade these big serpents to swallow a considerable number of plastic packets of drugs, whereas it is extremely diffcult to persuade a customs officer to reach into a sack containing several hundred live snakes and peer down the throat of each one of them to check for illegal substances.

This Toucan my man, is dead, stone cold, deceased!. finished' But tell me pray, why does he keep flying around my room?

UNDERCOVER COCKROACHES

In recent years the CIA has gained a reputation for employing all kinds of dubious lowlife in its illicit activities. Just how low this life has been, however, was probably not fully grasped until one researcher revealed the ultimate CIA recruit: the tracker cockroach.

The concept was based on 24 years of obscure research by a Dutch chemist who synthesized the hormone of the female cockroach. It was found that the scent from 1/100 of a gramme of this hormone, called periplanone-B, was sufficient to sexually excite 100 million male cockroaches. The idea was to use sexual attraction as a means of pest control, but researchers for the CIA had another plan.

It seems that anyone sprayed or dabbed with this substance could be sniffed out by means of a small container of male cockroaches which had been wired for sound. Evidently, when sexually excited, cockroaches emit high-frequency squeals that can be picked up and amplified so they can be heard by the human ear. Once marked by the scent, there is evidently no hiding from the insect posse.

Strangely enough, the new style 'bugging' researchers made no suggestions for other uses of the substance. On the face of it, it would seem to have far greater possibilities as an instrument of psychological torture. The idea of suddenly becoming the object of sexual desire for 100 million cockroaches is a terrifying, skin-crawling thought.

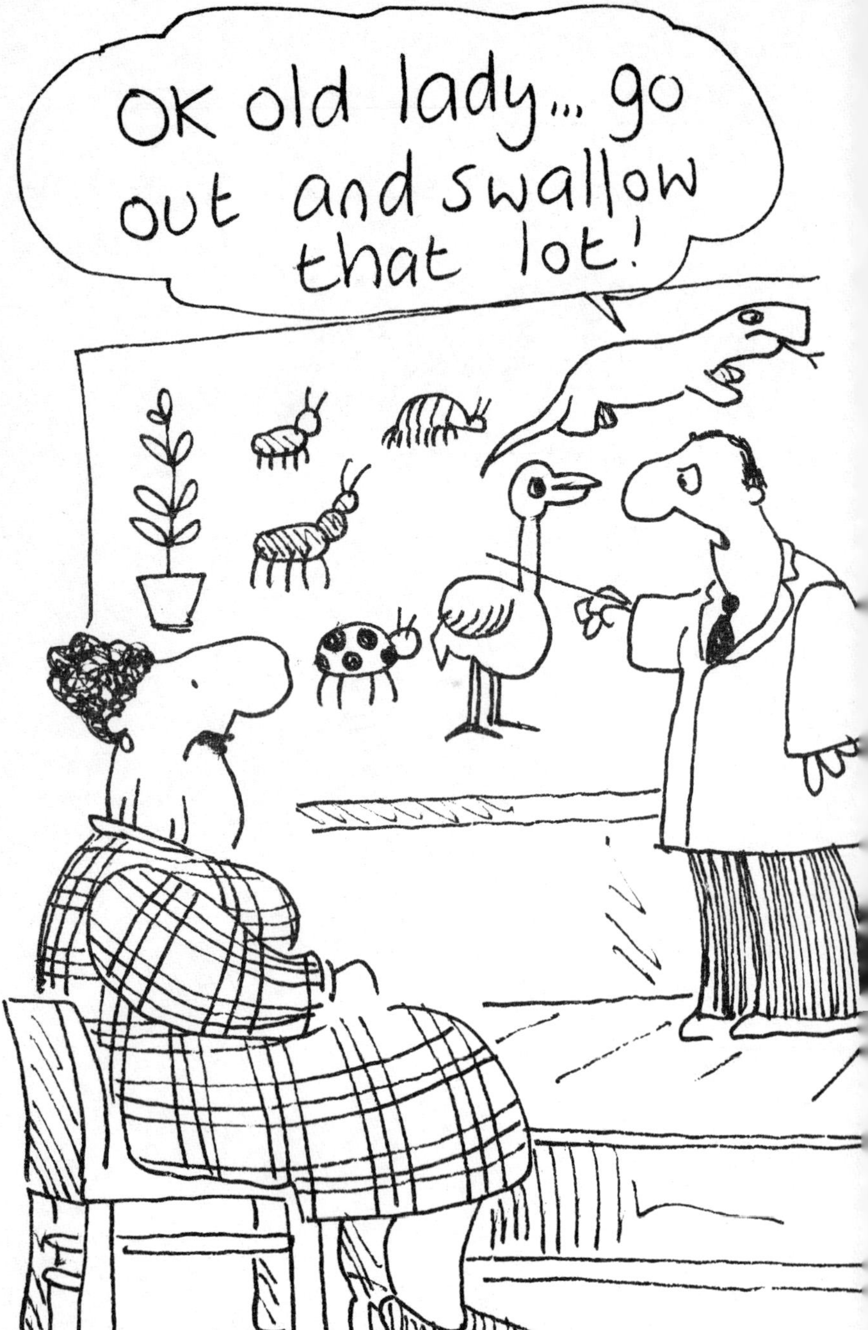
OK old lady... go out and swallow that lot!

VICIOUS CIRCLES

In 1946, a batch of ornamental nursery plants infested with a scale insect were imported into Bermuda. The insects promptly attacked the indigenous cedar trees. By 1951, 85% of all Bermuda's cedars were dead or dying. To control the insect the government introduced ladybird beetles and parasitic hymenoptera, both of which feed on these insects. Unfortunately someone had already imported angus lizards to control two species of previously introduced ants. It turned out that angus lizards, and both species of ants, loved nothing better than to dine on ladybirds and hymenoptera.

Escalating the conflict, the government then decided to control the lizards by bringing in the kiskadee, a West Indian lizard-eating bird. In 1956, two hundred kiskadees were released in the hope that the birds would eat the lizards that ate the ladybirds that were supposed to eat the scale insects that killed the cedars. Of course, there was a hitch. It turned out that kiskadees found native Bermudan white-eyed vireo nestlings much more to their liking than the lizards.

Subsequently, the kiskadees have increased to over 100,000. These are decimating the native vireo flocks quite as effectively as the lizards are wiping out the ladybirds and the ants are clobbering the hymenoptera and the scale insects are ravaging the Bermuda cedar. It is a typical scenario for the ever-multiplying problems created by randomly introduced species: a plot lifted straight out of the children's nursery song: 'There Was An Old Lady Who Swallowed A Fly'.

VULTURE POST

During the Vietnam War, the U.S. Airforce commissioned research into 'Airborne Biological Reconnaissance Systems'. In layman's terms the ABRS was a bird trained as a spy, or in colloquial terms: 'stool pigeon'. Fitted with microtransmitters, pigeons were trained to fly ahead of U.S. jungle patrols and spot any enemy lying in ambush. Although theoretically practical, the ABRS's seemed to have been entirely wiped out by a combination of Vietnamese pigeon pox and hungry Vietnamese villagers who would rather eat pigeon than almost anything. However, ABRS scientists did not restrict themselves to pigeon 'systems'. Starlings, crows, ducks, geese and finally, turkey vultures, were trained to demonstrate a capacity for delivering specialised or heavy packets and supplies to soldiers trapped in jungle war-zones. However, the reason for lack of widespread use of these particular ABRS had more to do with human psychology than practicality. One might wonder at how the morale of surrounded and entrenched soldiers in a combat-zone might be affected, for instance, if central command's messages were constantly conveyed by a vulture. Useful as it may have proved, the vulture-post was soon declared a dead letter.

WARRIOR DOVES

In a municipal park in the French textile town of Lille, there stands one of the world's most unusual monuments to the war dead. What makes it so unique is the nature of the thousands of war dead it commemorates as fallen heroes. It appears that in the course of the First and Second World Wars, some twenty thousand carrier pigeons were killed serving as couriers for the Allied armies of Europe. This monument in Lille was built to commemorate these sacrificed doves of war.

There are many stories of men and armies who have owed their survival to the success or failure of carrier pigeons making their way through enemy lines. Among the most famous in the First World War was the pigeon called 'Cher Ami'. This bird sustained seven wounds yet still managed to deliver a vital message before expiring. In doing so, she saved New York's 77th Division – later called the 'Lost Battalion' – from certain annihilation in its eleventh hour.

Upon her death, 'Cher Ami' was lovingly embalmed and is now enshrined in the American Smithsonian Institute in Washington, a small feathered monument to a critical time in human history.

WHOOPING CRANE AEROBICS

'If you've seen fifteen whooping cranes, you've seen them all.' In 1941, this statement was literally true. By 1962, despite elaborate protection policies, there were still only twenty-eight. Although the situation is much improved today with nearly three hundred birds in existence, conservationists have learned that every whooping crane counts. With this in mind, crane researcher George Archibald became involved with a particularly difficult female whooping crane named Tex. Tex had been orphaned and raised in captivity by humans. It soon became apparent that Tex grew up thinking of herself as more of a person than a crane, and proved not in the least interested in male cranes. Unfortunately, ordinary artificial insemination methods do not work with cranes. Females must perform an elaborate and rather exhausting ritual mating dance with a male in order to enter a fertile condition before insemination can occur.

All was not lost, however. Although absolutely refusing to dance with male whoopers, it was found that Tex was magnetically attracted to George Archibald, and with only a little encouragement, Tex proved more than happy to dance with the ornithologist.

In 1981, these intensive pre-natal aerobics finally paid off. Archibald lived with Tex in her marshy home for six weeks. For four of these he danced with her several times a day. He also foraged for twigs to help Tex build her nest. Finally Tex laid an egg and two weeks later it hatched. The little whooper, surviving its unorthodox upbringing, was named Gee Whiz by his proud foster father.

X-RATED MONKEYS

In 1970, the psychologists Beatrice and Allan Gardner, introduced the public to 'Washoe', the world's first 'talking' chimpanzee. Washoe learned to 'speak' by learning Ameslan or ASL (American Sign Language), the language of the deaf and dumb. Washoe's language skills astonished everyone. Washoe acquired a working vocabulary of 160 'words' and was carrying on two-way 'conversations' with humans.

Beyond learning the names of things, Washoe was able to 'read' questions, construct sentences and make demands. At first these were limited to the 'Gimme food' or 'Gimme drink' kind, but the statements became increasingly complex. She would take her humans to the refrigerator and make the signs: 'Open food drink'. Addressing her trainer, Roger Fouts, she often requested: 'Roger Washoe tickle', She also showed an ability to create new word combinations, such as calling duck a 'water bird'.

It often seemed to her trainer that Washoe made chimp jokes of sorts, which she usually confirmed by signing: 'Funny'. She generally exhibited a preference for 'toilet humour', and she tended to use 'toilet words' as a means of cursing: the sign of faeces and urine being the most popular. When Washoe became irritated by a particularly annoying rhesus monkey, she often signed 'shit monkey' or even 'green shit monkey'.

YEMENI RHINOS

The highest-priced trophy animal these days is the rhinoceros. However, it is no longer big-game trophy hunters who pose the major threat to the existence of this second largest of all land animals. Its fate is now in the hands of specialized markets, virtually unknown to the world at large until the late 1970s.

One is a unique tradition in South Yemen, where the sons of the wealthiest aristocrats are presented with ceremonial daggers made with rhinoceros horn handles. Once such daggers, called jambias, were only available to a handful of aristocrats, but with the influx of wealth from the Saudi oilfields, every Yemeni youth whose family can afford it receives a rhino horn dagger as a status symbol. Consequently rhinoceros horn has soared astronomically – a single horn is now reputed to be selling at more than $24,000.

The other major market is the Chinese pseudo-pharmaceutical market; part of which deals in aphrodisiacs and aids to male potency. This market willingly pays over $600 a kilo for powder ground from African rhino horn shavings, while powder from the almost extinct Asian rhino is valued at $6,500 a kilo. Entire Asian rhino horns have a retail value in excess of $40,000. Today, Taiwan has become the centre of the rhino horn market. Its close links with South Africa have allowed a smugglers' pipeline to be established.

Rugged to the point of appearing almost invincible, the rhinoceros in its armour-like skin has survived seventy million years of evolution, and a million years or more of human predation. Yet, all five species are now critically endangered. It remains to be seen if this formidable animal can survive a few decades of free enterprise trade in what amounts to a high-priced fad-and-fashion market.

ZORRO OF THE GREENS

The Washington-based anti-pollution group Environmental Action is generally credited in the late Sixties for coining the term 'Ecotage' to describe non-violent ecological sabotage. However, it was Illinois that produced the world's first true 'ecotage commando'.

This rebel with a cause has never been unmasked, but during the early Sixties, he was known as 'The Fox' of Kane County, Illinois. Mike Royko, *Chicago Daily Express* columnist who was the Fox's media contact, described him as 'an anti-pollution Zorro who has been harassing various companies, evading the police and making himself a minor legend'. In his various escapades, and wearing many disguises, he appeared in corporation offices and buildings to deliver the sludge and dead fish that were the by-products of their particular industries. Elsewhere the Fox blocked factory sewage and drainage systems, and sealed off smokestacks. Wherever he struck, he always left a note of explanation, advising the company to 'clean up their act' and signing it 'The Fox'. These actions were usually followed up by a poster campaign against the offending corporation.

The Fox of the Sixties was the prototype for the environmental protesters of the Seventies and Eighties who are most typically identified with such groups as Greenpeace. The Fox's techniques are now standard practice for the ecological urban guerilla. At one stage it seemed that every city in Europe and America had a stream of activists scaling its industrial smokestacks to hang protest banners. One newspaper went so far as nominating smokestack–climbing as a new Olympic sporting event. Such is the heritage of the Fox.